Choosing My Religion

For Lisa +
Scott

Choosing My Religion

Religion

A Memoir of a Family

Beyond Belief

Stephen J. Dubner

HARPER ● PERENNIAL

NEW YORK ● LONDON ● TORONTO ● SYDNEY

HARPER ● PERENNIAL

A hardcover edition of this book was published under the title *Turbulent Souls* in 1998 by William Morrow, an imprint of HarperCollins Publishers.

P.S.™ is a trademark of HarperCollins Publishers.

HarperCollins books may be purchased for educational, business, or sales promotional use. For information, please e-mail the Special Markets Department at SPsales@harpercollins.com.

First Bard edition published 1999.

First Harper Perennial edition published 2006.

Designed by Jo Anne Metsch

The Library of Congress has catalogued the hardcover edition as follows:

Dubner, Stephen J.
    Turbulent Souls : a Catholic son's return to his Jewish family / Stephen J. Dubner.
        p. cm.
    ISBN 0-380-72930-X
     1. Dubner, Stephen J. 2. Dubner, Veronica. 3. Dubner, Paul. 4. Converts from Judaism—United States—Biography. 5. Proselytes and proselyting, Jewish—Converts from Christianity—Biography. 6. Jews—United States—Biography.
I. Title.
    BM729.P7D83 1998
    248.2'46'0922—dc21

                98-34077
                CIP

ISBN-10: 0-06-113299-3 (pbk.)
ISBN-13: 978-0-06-113299-5 (pbk.)

15 RRD 10 9 8 7 6 5 4